UNLOCKING THE SECRETS OF THE DASHOPANISHADS

A CONCISE VIEW TO THE ANCIENT WISDOM

DR. JAGADEESH PILLAI

|| Dedicated to All Wisdom Seekers Around The World ||

Contents

Prayer   *vii*

About The Author   *ix*

Preface   *xiii*

Part 1

  1. Isha Upanishad   3

Part 2

  2. Kena Upanishad   11

Part 3

  3. Katha Upanishad   17

Part 4

  4. Prashna Upanishad   23

Part 5

  5. Mundaka Upanishad   37

Part 6

  6. Mandukya Upanishad   43

Part 7

  7. Taittiriya Upanishad   47

Part 8

  8. Aitareya Upanishad   53

Part 9

  9. Chandogya Upanishad   59

Part 10

  10. Brihadaranyaka Upanishad   69

Other Books Of The Author   79

Contents

Contact   83

PRAYER

**"Om Poornamadah Poornamidam Poornat
Poornamudachyate,Poornasya Poornamaadaya
Poornamevavavashishyate,Om Shantih, Shantih, Shantih"**

*The literal interpretation of this mantra is: That which is
Absolute, This which is Absolute, Absolute arises from Absolute,
If Absolute is removed from Absolute, Absolute remains.
OM Peace, Peace, Peace.*

ABOUT THE AUTHOR

Dr. Jagadeesh Pillai is a renowned Guinness World Record holder, writer, and researcher hailing from Varanasi, also known as the abode of Lord Shiva. With a Ph.D. in Vedic Science and a range of creative ideas and achievements, he is a true polymath. He is the author of more than 100 books including Research Publications. Although his roots can be traced back to Kerala, the people of Varanasi hold him in high regard and affectionately consider him one of their own.

Dr. Pillai has achieved four Guinness World Records in the following subjects:

"Script to Screen" - In this record, Dr. Pillai produced and directed an animation film within the shortest time possible, breaking the previous record set by Canadians. He has also received numerous national and international awards and recognitions for this achievement.

Longest Line of Postcards - For this record, Dr. Pillai created a line of 16,300 postcards on the occasion of the 163rd anniversary of Indian Postal Day. The event also included a questionnaire about the Indian flag.

Largest Poster Awareness Campaign - Dr. Pillai designed an awareness campaign on the subject of "Beti Bachao - Beti Padhao" (Save the Girl Child - Educate the Girl Child) to achieve this record.

Largest Envelope - In tribute to the Indian Prime Minister's

"Make in India" initiative, Dr. Pillai created a 4000 square meter envelope using waste paper to achieve this record.

Attempted - **70000 Candles on a 210 kg Cake** - To celebrate the 70th Indian Independence Day, Dr. Pillai attempted to light 70,000 candles on a 210 kg cake, which was recorded in World Records India.

Attempted - **Documentary on Dhamek Stupa of Sarnath in 17 Languages** - Dr. Pillai attempted to create a documentary on the Dhamek Stupa of Sarnath, dubbing it in 17 different languages. The result of this attempt is currently awaiting confirmation from the Guinness World Records.

Dr. Pillai is skilled in teaching the Bhagavad Gita, a Hindu scripture, and is popular among young people. He has helped many young people improve their lives through his motivational teachings.

In addition to teaching, he has composed and sung numerous Sanskrit Bhajans and patriotic songs.

He has also written and directed several short films and documentaries for awareness campaigns, and has volunteered with the police in both UP and Kerala to spread awareness about various issues through videos and photography.

Incredibly, he has produced and directed over 100 documentaries about the city of Varanasi, all on his own.

He has also helped and guided more than 25 boys and girls to achieve world records through creative and innovative methods. He is a multifaceted person who uses his intellect and the blessings given to him by God to excel in various areas. He is both a teacher and a student, always learning and teaching, and is able to master any subject he comes across.

He is a selfless social activist and motivational speaker who has overcome struggles and failures to become a successful and enthusiastic individual with a rich life experience.

In addition to his work with the Bhagavad Gita, he is also an efficient Tarot card reader, Astro-Vastu consultant, and a talented singer and composer. He has sung the entire Ram Charita Manas and Bhagavad Gita in his own compositions, and has sung the phrase "Lokah Samastha Sukhino Bhavantu" in 50 different languages. He is currently working on a detailed and scientific study of Vedas, Upanishads, Puranas, and the Bhagavad Gita. He has also composed and sung the Hanuman Chalisa and Gayatri Mantra in 108 and 1008 different compositions, respectively.

Awards - Four Times Guinness World Records, Winner of Mahatma Gandhi Vishwa Shanti Puraskar, Mahatma Gandhi Global Peace Ambassador, Kashi Ratna Award, Dr. APJ Abdul Kalam Motivational Person of the Year 2017, Mother Teresa Award, Indira Gandhi Priyadarshini Award, Bharat Vikas Ratna Award, Udyog Ratna Award, Vigyan Prasar Award, Poorvanchal Ratn Samman.

Preface

The Upanishads are ancient texts that contain some of the central philosophical concepts of Hinduism, Buddhism, and Jainism. They form the core of the Vedanta school of Hindu philosophy, and they have also been highly influential in the development of other Indian religions and philosophies. In this book, "**Unlocking the Secrets of the Dashopanishads**," I have provided a brief overview of each of the 10 Upanishads: Ishavasyopanishad, Kenopanishad, Kathopanishad, Prashnopanishad, Mundakopanishad, Mandukyopanishad, Taitiriyopanishad, Aitareyopanishad, Chandogyopanishad, and Brihadaranyopanishad.

The Upanishads are traditionally passed down orally, and they contain teachings on a wide range of topics, including the nature of ultimate reality, the self, consciousness, and the relationship between the individual soul and the ultimate divine reality. They are considered to be the foundation of Vedantic philosophy, and they have also had a profound impact on Buddhism, Jainism and various other spiritual traditions.

This book is not intended to be a comprehensive guide to the Upanishads, but rather a brief introduction to the main ideas and concepts found in each of the texts. I have aimed to present the Upanishads in a way that is accessible to readers who are new to these texts, while also providing enough detail to give readers a sense of the depth and complexity of the Upanishads.

I believe that reading the Upanishads, even in brief form,

can be a valuable and enlightening experience. These ancient texts contain wisdom that is still relevant today, and they offer a unique perspective on the nature of reality, the self, and the ultimate goal of human existence. I hope that this book will serve as a helpful introduction to these texts, and that it will inspire readers to delve deeper into the Upanishads and the rich philosophical tradition they represent.

In conclusion, **"Unlocking the Secrets of the Dashopanishads"** is a collection of brief summaries of each Upanishads as to give a brief idea about the content in each Upanishad. It is not a comprehensive study on Upanishads but just a brief overview. The Upanishads are profound texts that have been influential in the spiritual traditions of India, and they contain teachings that are still relevant today. Reading this book may be a valuable and enlightening experience and it will inspire readers to delve deeper into the Upanishads and the rich philosophical tradition they represent.

"Om Poornamadah Poornamidam Poornat Poornamudachyate,Poornasya Poornamaadaya Poornamevavavashishyate,Om Shantih, Shantih, Shantih"

The literal interpretation of this mantra is: That which is Absolute, This which is Absolute, Absolute arises from Absolute, If Absolute is removed from Absolute, Absolute remains.

OM Peace, Peace, Peace.

I

Isha Upanishad

The Isha Upanishad is a Mukhya Upanishad, which means that it is considered to be one of the primary and most important Upanishads in Hinduism. It is embedded as the final chapter of the Shukla Yajurveda, and is known in two recensions, called Kanva and Madhyandina. The Upanishad is a brief poem, consisting of 17 or 18 verses, depending on the recension.

The Isha Upanishad is renowned for its singular mention of the term Isha in the first hymn, a term that is never repeated in the other hymns. Depending on the interpretation, Isha can be seen as representing monism or a form of monotheism, referred to as Self or Deity Lord respectively. The term This All is the empirical reality, while the term renounced is referring to the Indian concept of sannyasa, and enjoy thyself is referring to the blissful delight of Self-realization.

The Advaita Vedanta scholar Shankara interprets the hymn as equating the Lord to the Atman (Self). In contrast,

Madhvacharya, the Dvaita Vedanta scholar, interprets the hymn as equating the Lord to Vishnu, or a monotheistic God in a henotheistic sense. Other interpretations have also been suggested, such as the more recent scholar Mahīdhara's suggestion that hymn 1 may be referring to Buddha. However, Max Muller argued that this interpretation was inadmissible due to the fundamental differences between Hinduism and Buddhism, with Hinduism relying on the premise of Self existing and Buddhism relying on the premise of Self not existing.

The Isha Upanishad, in hymns 2–6, acknowledges the contrasting tension within Hinduism between the empirical life of a householder and action (karma) and the spiritual life of renunciation and knowledge (jnana). It states that if one wishes to live a hundred years on this earth, they should do so by engaging in karma. Those who partake in the nature of the Asuras (evil) are enveloped in blind darkness, and that is where they reside who ignore their Atman (Self). To achieve liberation, one must know their Atman, which is motionless yet faster than the mind, distant yet near, within all and without all. He who beholds all beings in the Self, and the Self in all beings, will never turn away from it (the Self).

Adi Shankara suggests that the seeker of emancipation in hymn 6 is on a journey to realize Self and Oneness in their innermost self and everyone, and includes those in sannyasa; while Madhvacharya suggests he is the individual Self in loving devotion of God, seeking to get infinitely close to the God Self.

The Isha Upanishad teaches that the root of sorrow and

suffering is the belief in a separate self, separate from the selves of others. This belief in duality leads to the assumption that one's happiness and suffering is distinct from that of others. The Upanishad suggests that this suffering can be overcome by realizing that the self is in all things, understanding the oneness of existence, and focusing on universal values rather than individual egos.

The Upanishad also presents the concept of Vidya (real knowledge, eternal truths) and Avidya (not real knowledge, empirical truths). It states that one who knows both Vidya and Avidya will be empowered with the ability to overcome death through Avidya and attain immortality through Vidya. Real knowledge leads to liberation from all sorrows and fears, and a blissful state of life.

In the later hymns, the Upanishad advises against the pursuit of only material or spiritual causes, stating that one-sided pursuits lead to darkness. Instead, it suggests seeking both material and spiritual knowledge to achieve enlightenment. The Upanishad asserts that one who understands both the Real and the Perishable, both the manifested not-true cause and the hidden true cause, will be liberated unto immortality. The Upanishad is recommending that one must pursue material knowledge and spiritual wisdom simultaneously, and that a fulfilling life results from the harmonious, balanced alignment of the individual and the social interests, the personal and the organizational goals, the material and the spiritual pursuits of life.

In the final hymns of the Isha Upanishad, the text asserts the importance of knowledge and self-reflection. It states that knowledge is hidden behind a golden disc of light, but that one should seek it and remember one's actions and accept their consequences. The Madhyandina and Kanva recensions of the Upanishad present variations in the sequence of these hymns, but both include the introspective precept of asking the fire and mind to lead one towards a virtuous life and away from a life of vices. This will guide one towards the good path and the enjoyment of wealth, both in the form of material rewards and spiritual realization.

The final hymns of the Isha Upanishad also present the foundational premise of the text, "I am He," equating the oneness of the individual self with the cosmic self. This teaching encourages the reader to see the underlying unity in all things and to understand the oneness of existence, which leads to the transcendence of duality and the realization of the self.

Despite its brevity, the Isha Upanishad is considered to be one of the most profound and influential Upanishads in Hinduism. It is revered for its insights into the nature of reality and the ultimate goal of human life, and is often studied and revered by spiritual seekers and practitioners of yoga and meditation.

One of the key themes of the Isha Upanishad is the concept of **Brahman**, which is the ultimate reality and the ultimate goal of human life. According to the Upanishad, Brahman is the ultimate source of all existence, and is the ultimate goal of all spiritual pursuits. It is described as being infinite, eternal, and all-pervading, and is beyond the limitations of time and space.

Another key theme of the Isha Upanishad is the concept of **Atman**, which is the individual soul or self. According to the Upanishad, the Atman is a spark of the divine, and is an essential part of the ultimate reality of Brahman. The Upanishad teaches that the ultimate goal of human life is to realize the unity of the Atman and Brahman, and to merge with the ultimate reality of the universe.

The Isha Upanishad also emphasizes the importance of yoga and meditation in the spiritual journey. It teaches that through the practice of yoga and meditation, the individual can cultivate a deep inner peace and stillness, and can come to a realization of the unity of the Atman and Brahman.

The Isha Upanishad is a powerful and influential text that has had a profound impact on Hinduism and the spiritual traditions of India. Its teachings on the nature of reality, the ultimate goal of human life, and the importance of yoga and meditation have inspired and influenced countless spiritual seekers over the centuries, and continue to do so to this day.

**"Om Aapyaayantu Mamaangaani
VaakPraanashchakshuh ShrotramathoBalamindriyaani
Cha Sarvaani Sarvam BrahmopanishadamMaaham
Brahma Niraakuryaam Maa Maa Brahma
NiraakarodNiraakaranamastva Niraakaranam Me
AstuTadaatmani Nirate Ya Upanishatsu
DharmaasteMayi Santu Te Mayi SantuOm Shantih,
Shantih, Shantih"**

The Mantra implies: OM. May our organs, speech, Prana,
eyes, and ears be nourished and strengthened. The
Upanishads proclaim that the entire world is Brahman.
We do not reject Brahman, and may Brahma not reject us.
Let us strive to ensure that there is no rejection within us,
and let us focus on living a righteous life as prescribed by
the Upanishads. Be in us,

OM Peace, Peace, and Peace.

ॐ

II

Kena Upanishad

The Kenopanishad is part of the Samavedic corpus, comprising the ninth chapter of the Brahmana. It is also known as Talavakara Upanishad or the Brahmanopanishad. The name of the Upanishad, "Kena," is derived from the opening word of the text, which is "kena," meaning "by whom." This Upanishad is focused on the knowledge of the Pure and Unconditioned Brahman, or Suddha Brahman, as opposed to the earlier chapters that dealt with the karmas (ritualistic actions) and upasanas (worship) of the conditioned Brahman, also known as Prana. The author of this Upanishad follows the commentary of Adi Sankara, a well-known philosopher and commentator of the Upanishads, in interpreting its teachings. It begins with the question "Kenesit... (Who impels this life?)" From this question, it is referred to as Kenopanishad. The sage, while extolling the glory of Parabrahma and its form, has clearly stated that the Brahman is as subtle as it is distant from the realm of speech and hearing.

The first and second sections describe the special qualities of the inspiring sage, his realization, and the necessity of knowing him in beautiful language.

The third and fourth sections mention the manifestation of Brahman in the form of Yajna in the form of Brahmani consciousness and the description of Brahman by Uma Devi.

Finally, the description of the glory of knowing the mystery with the resources of Brahman Vidya is mentioned at the end.

The third section of Kena Upanishad, is presented as a fable and is an allegory, and is considered one of the most profound passages in the text. The fable begins with a war between gods and demons in which the Brahman, the ultimate reality and cosmic principle in Hinduism, emerges victorious. However, the gods take credit for the victory and do not recognize the Brahman.

The gods then send god Agni (fire) to investigate this mysterious being. Agni rushes to the Brahman and is asked "who are you?" Agni replies, "I am Agni, knower of beings." The Brahman then asks Agni about the source of his power, and Agni replies, "I am able to burn whatever is on earth." The Brahman then presents a piece of grass and challenges Agni to burn it, but Agni is unable to do so. He returns to the gods and tells them that he cannot discover what this being is.

The gods then sent god Vayu (air) to investigate and he too rushes to the Brahman. The Brahman asks Vayu "who are you?" and Vayu replies, "I am Vayu, I am Matarisvan (what fills the aerial space around mother earth, mover in space)." Like Agni, Vayu is asked about the source of his power and replies, "I am able to carry or pull whatever is on earth." The Brahman then presents a piece of grass and challenges Vayu to carry it away, but Vayu is unable to do so. He returns to the gods and tells them that he cannot discover what this being is.

The gods then turn to god Indra (lightning, god of might) to investigate. When he reaches the Brahman, he finds a beautiful woman with knowledge named Umā. Indra asks Umā "what is this wonderful being?" and Umā replies, "that is the Brahman; that is the one who obtained victory, though gods praise themselves for it." With this revelation, Indra understands the true nature of the being they had encountered. The tradition holds that Agni, Vayu and Indra are revered above all other gods because they were the first to "meet" and "experience" the Brahman, with Indra being the most celebrated for having "known" the Brahman first among all gods.

"Om Sahanaa Vavatu Sahanau BhunaktuSaha Veeryam KaravaavahaiTejasvi Naavadheetamastu Maa VidvishaavahaiOm Shantih Shantih Shantih"

The literal interpretation of this mantra is: OM. Let us all protect one another, let us all share in joy, let us all work together and let our learning be illuminated. Let us be united in peace,

OM Peace, Peace, Peace.

III

Katha Upanishad

The Katha Upanishad is part of the Krishna Yajurveda, consisting of two chapters and three sections in each. It is famously known for the dialogue between Nachiketa, the son of Vajashrava, and Yama. Vajashrava had asked Nachiketa to perform a yagna with unblemished objects as an offering. Nachiketa asked his father repeatedly what he should offer, to which his father replied that he should offer it to Yama.

When Nachiketa meets Yama, he is asked for three boons. In the first, he requests that his father be praised and respected, in the second, he asks for heavenly knowledge, and in the third, he requests knowledge of the Self. Yama grants him the first two boons, but tries to dissuade him from the third, as it is difficult to attain. This is the story of the first section of the first chapter.

The second chapter describes the attainment of the Supreme, His description, His abode in the heart, and various aspects of the Supreme such as His all-pervasiveness, the practice of yoga, faith in the Lord, and liberation. Finally, Nachiketa is said to have attained Brahman through the power of Brahman knowledge.

One of the main stories in the Kathopanishad revolves around the character of Nachiketa, a young boy who is curious about the nature of reality and the ultimate goal of human life. Nachiketa becomes disillusioned with the material world and the pursuit of wealth and power, and decides to seek out a deeper understanding of the ultimate nature of the self and the universe.

In the Katha Upanishad, a story is told of a boy named Nachiketa who visits the god of death, Yama. Nachiketa asks Yama to teach him about the nature of the self and the afterlife. Yama is impressed by the boy's intelligence and devotion, and agrees to teach him, but first offers him three boons as a reward for his visit.

The first boon that Nachiketa asks for is that his father, who had sent him to Yama as a sacrifice, may be reconciled with him. Yama grants this boon and Nachiketa's father is reconciled with him.

The second boon that Nachiketa asks for is to know the secret of fire, which will give him the power to create fire whenever he wants. Yama grants this boon as well and teaches Nachiketa about the nature of fire and how to create it.

The third boon that Nachiketa asks for is to know the secret of the afterlife, which will give him the knowledge of the self and the true nature of the soul. Yama grants this boon and teaches Nachiketa about the nature of the self, the soul, and the afterlife. He explains that the self is not the physical body, but rather an eternal, unchanging, and infinite consciousness that underlies all existence. He also explains that the soul is the eternal essence of a person, which continues on after death, and that the true nature of the soul is to be united with the ultimate reality.

In this story, Nachiketa is depicted as a very pure, sincere and intelligent boy, who is deeply committed to seeking the truth and knowledge. Yama, who is at first reluctant to teach Nachiketa, is impressed by his intelligence, devotion and purity. Through Nachiketa's quest for knowledge, the Upanishad conveys the idea that the true purpose of human life is to seek the knowledge of self and the ultimate reality, and that this knowledge will lead to freedom from the cycle of rebirth and union with the ultimate reality.

Yama teaches Nachiketa about the nature of reality and the ultimate goal of human life. He explains to Nachiketa that the ultimate goal of human life is to realize the unity of the Atman and Brahman, and to merge with the ultimate reality of the universe. He also teaches Nachiketa about the importance of ethical conduct and selfless action in the spiritual journey, and the need to cultivate a deep inner peace and stillness through the practice of yoga and meditation.

Through his teachings, Yama helps Nachiketa to gain a deeper understanding of the ultimate nature of reality and the ultimate goal of human life. Nachiketa becomes enlightened as a result of his interactions with Yama, and is able to achieve the ultimate goal of human life.

The story of Nachiketa and Yama in the Kathopanishad is a powerful and influential tale that has had a profound impact on Hinduism and the spiritual traditions of India. It teaches the importance of seeking out a deeper understanding of the ultimate nature of reality and the ultimate goal of human life.

**"Om Bhadram Karnebhih Shrunuyaama
DevaahBhadram Pashyemaakshabhiryajatraah
SthirairangaistushtuvaamsastanoobhihVyashema
Devahitam YadaayuhSwasti Na Indro
VridhashravaahSwasti Nah Pooshaa
VishwavedaahSwasti Nastaarkshyo ArishtanemihSwasti
No Brihaspatir DadhaatuOm Shantih, Shantih, Shantih"**

The literal meaning of this mantra is: OM. O Gods! Let us hear auspicious words from our ears. O reverent Gods! Let us behold propitious visions from our eyes, let our organs and body be stable, healthy, and strong. Let us do that which is pleasing to the gods in the life span allotted to us. May Indra, inscribed in the scriptures, bring us fortune! May Pushan, the knower of the world, grant us prosperity! May Trakshya, who vanquishes enemies, bestow us with blessings! May Brihaspati bring us success!

OM Peace, Peace, Peace.

IV
Prashna Upanishad

The Prashnopanishad is a Brahmana part of the Atharvaveda. It contains six questions asked by the seekers to Maharshi Pippalada and their answers.

The first question was to know about Prana and Rayi in Khanda.

The second question was asked by Bhargava with three questions related to the people.

In the third question, Ashtavakra asked six questions in the context of the origin of Prana.

The fourth question was asked by Gargya regarding the relationship between Jivatma and Paramatma with five questions.

The fifth question required knowledge of the worship of Om Kar in Satyakama.

The sixth question was asked by Sukesha, which included sixteen questions related to the Kalayukta Purusha.

Finally, all the questions were answered satisfactorily and the seekers expressed their gratitude to Maharshi Pippalada.

The Prashnopanishad is a text that provides an in-depth exploration of the mantras found in the Mundaka Upanishad. It is structured as a series of six questions and answers that delve into various aspects of ritual and meditation, as well as the ultimate goal and benefits of spiritual practice. The first three questions focus on the practical aspects of rites and meditation, including the benefits that can be achieved and the potential for excess or dissatisfaction. The fourth question delves into the concept of "Brahma Tatva," or the ultimate reality, while the fifth question explores the methods for achieving spiritual realization. The final question explores the ultimate realization of spiritual enlightenment. In this way, the Prashnopanishad provides a comprehensive and detailed understanding of the teachings found in the Mundaka Upanishad.

1st question

The first question of the Prashnopanishad is related to the extensive and intensive aspects of Rites and Meditation, and also the fruits, even to the consequent surfeit and perhaps of repugnance. The question is asked by the sage

Pippalada to the great seer and spiritual master, Sri Sanatkumara. The answer provided by Sri Sanatkumara not only delves into the nature of the Rites and Meditation, but also provides insight into the nature of the fruits and the potential for excess or dissatisfaction that one may encounter in the spiritual practice. The main theme of the answer is the idea of balance and moderation in spiritual practice.

In the answer, it is explained that Prajapati, who is responsible for the creation and sustenance of the universe, cogitated the Vedic way as Hiranyagarbha, by his erstwhile thoughts of ability to create. He generated rayim (food) and praanam (life energy) to sustain the cycle of existence. It's said that Moon or Food and Agni or Surya the Praana the vital force are the foundation of all existence and it's through their interaction that the universe comes into being and continues to exist.

Additionally, the answer explains that while performing the rituals and meditation one must be careful not to become attached to the fruits of their practice, as this can lead to surfeit and dissatisfaction, instead one must strive for balance and moderation in their spiritual practice. As the ultimate goal should be the realization of the ultimate reality and attaining the state of liberation, and not the temporary fruits or pleasures that one may gain from the practices.

Furthermore, the answer stresses the importance of seeking guidance from a qualified teacher or guru, who can guide the individual in the right direction and provide insight into the true nature of the practices and the fruits that can be gained. It's said that this guidance is necessary as it's easy to get lost in the temporary pleasures and become attached to them, neglecting the ultimate goal.

The first question of the Prashnopanishad provides a wealth of spiritual and philosophical insight into the nature of Rites and Meditations, their fruits, and the potential for excess or dissatisfaction. Through its answer, it emphasizes the importance of understanding the true nature of the practices and fruits, and the ultimate goal of attaining the state of liberation. It also stresses the importance of moderation and guidance of a qualified teacher in one's spiritual practice.

2nd question

The Second Question in the Prashnopanishad concerns the prime supports of life and the body, with Praana as their binding force. Bhargav, a student of the sage Pippalaada, asks about the different powers that sustain and shine in the universe, and which one is considered the most outstanding. Pippalaada responds by listing the different elements that support and sustain the universe: Akasha (ether), Vaayu (wind), Agni (fire), Aapah (water), Prithivi (earth), Vaak (speech), Manas (mind), Chakshu (eyes), and Shrotram (ears). He also emphasizes that the body acts as a binding entity that combines these organs and senses together, ensuring that they work in harmony and that there is no disintegration.

Praana is then identified as the magnificent power house that controls and coordinates the body parts and senses. It explains that the body cannot claim that the binding energy of existence should be itself and nothing else. Praana further explains that it would divide itself into five different types of energy: Praana, Apaana, Vyaana, Udaana, and Samaana, and assigns their duties accordingly, ensuring that the body parts and senses would not get disintegrated.

Praana further emphasizes that as soon as the mind of the body gets irritated, Praana would be roused and ascended, and on gaining normalcy would remain in position, just as the king of bees would take to furious flight, his army of bees would fly off around making a buzzing noise, and later on as the king settles, the army settles too. Similarly, the body parts like speech, eyes, ears, and tongue act and react accordingly.

Finally, Praana is compared to the hub of a chariot, with various extensions of knowledge and its instruments of action fixed on it, such as the Rigveda, Yajurveda, and Saama Veda, Yajnas, Kshatriyas, and Brahmanas. It is stated that Praana being the source of life, all being are dependent on it. The text emphasized the importance of understanding of this underlying power that sustains and supports all living beings, which is Praana.

3rd Question

The Third Question of the Prashnopanishad delves into the topic of the origin, sustenance, and eventual departure of human life, and how it is connected to the individual self. The enquirer, Kaushalya, asks Pippalaada Maharshi about the source of human life, how it enters the body, how it distributes itself within the body, and its external supports. Pippalaada acknowledges the deep and mystical nature of the question and states that the enquirer must be a true seeker of Brahman.

He then explains that the source of human life is the Atman, or inner consciousness, and it is generated by the actions of the mind and body. He also states that it is Mundaka Upanishad, another ancient Indian text, which also describes that the Atman is the source of human life. The Upanishad describes the Atman as formless, unborn, and self-effulgent, residing within the individual and without.

Pippalaada also describes how Praana distributes itself within the body, stating that it enters through the body's organs and senses, such as the eyes and ears, and settles in the heart. The Praana also has five different aspects, Apaana, Vyaana, Udaana, and Samaana, which work together to ensure that the body and its organs and senses function properly and remain connected. He further explains that the Praana also controls the body's energy and sustenance, and that it is the Praana which enables the body to act and react accordingly, for example, in case mind get irritated.

Pippalaada concludes that Praana, the life force, is a powerful force that sustains and controls the human body and is closely connected to the Atman or the individual self. It is the binding energy of existence that ensures the continuity of life and its connection to the individual self. He also emphasizes that this question is profound and only a true seeker of Brahman should be asking such question.

4th Question

In the fourth question of Prashnopanishad, Sauryaayani Gargyah asks Pippalaada Maharshi about the details of the physical limbs that are rested in the condition of deep sleep and kept awake in the concerned person, and whether there is any extraordinary force visualized in the dream stage. He further asks whether that divine force would drive the individual to joy and what details could be provided in this context. Pippalaada explains that in the dream stage, the mind of the person becomes unified and cannot hear, see, smell, taste, touch, speak, understand, enjoy, reject or move about. He further explains that praana, agni, apaana, vyaana and samaana control the body in different ways during the dream stage and that there is a divine force that controls the experiences of the individual in the dream state. This force is responsible for the person experiencing what they see, hear, and understand in their dream, and it allows them to experience various places and events even though they are physically at rest. Overall, Pippalaada suggests that this force is responsible for the person's mind and body to experience everything in the dream state, whether it is seen or unseen, heard or unheard, experienced or unexperienced.

The Fourth Question: In the dream stage what controls body faculties! -The Mind or the Soul?

Gargya, the grandson of Surya, posed a series of questions to Maharshi Pippalaada regarding the physical and mental state of an individual during deep sleep and in the dream stage. He enquired about the specific limbs that are at rest during deep sleep and active during the dream stage. Additionally, he asked whether there is an extraordinary force present in the dream stage that drives the individual to joy and if further details could be provided in this context. Gargya also referred to an Unknown Immutable and Absolute Force, which was perhaps beyond comprehension yet beneficent, and this is hinted in Mundaka Upanishad II.i.1. Pippalaada replied that just as the rays of the setting sun become unified in the Solar Orbit and scatter again at sunrise, the mind of the person in the dream stage is not able to hear, see, smell, taste, touch, speak, understand, enjoy, reject or move about and that one would think that the person has fallen asleep.

Pippalaada further explained that during deep sleep, the three fire principles known as Garhapatya, Ahavaniya, and Dakshina are awake in the body, each responsible for different functions. The Garhapatya principle is responsible for digestion, the Ahavaniya principle takes care of inhalation and exhalation, and the Dakshina principle is responsible for the assimilation of food and the transformation of matter. Additionally, the Samaana principle ensures an equal distribution of the life force throughout the body. The mind is the one that performs the sacrifice and it is also the one that receives the desired result of the sacrifice. Through these sacrifices, the mind reaches the ultimate reality of Brahman. During the dream state, the individual experiences the power and greatness of this divine force. It sees what is seen and hears what is heard and it experiences everything that is seen, unseen, heard and unheard, true and untrue, in all places and at all times. This is the nature and power of the mind during the dream state.

In summary, Pippalaada explains to Gargya that the mind is the primary controlling force during the dream stage.

The praana, or life force, is present, but it is the mind that experiences and perceives the dream. He uses the analogy of the rays of the setting sun becoming unified in the solar orbit before scattering again at sunrise to explain that the mind of the person in the dream stage is not able to process sensory input, such as hearing, seeing, smelling, tasting, touching, speaking, understanding, enjoying, rejecting or moving about, which would make the person seem to be in deep sleep. Pippalaada also stated that during the dream stage, mind experiences the sense of divinity, can see and hear things both seen and unseen, known and unknown, in different places and everything perceived by mind as true.

In the dream stage, it is the mind that controls the body faculties and not the soul. Pippalaada explains that when a person is in deep sleep, the praana, or life force, and all the other physical limbs become unified, similar to how the rays of the setting sun become unified in the solar orbit. The mind of the person in the dream stage cannot hear, see, smell, taste, touch, speak, understand, enjoy, reject or move about, and one may think that the person is asleep. However, the mind still experiences and perceives things in the dream state. The mind is the one that sees the dream, experiences it and remembers it. The mind experiences different places, people and events in the dream, though they may not always be the same as in the waking state. The mind is able to experience both the seen and the unseen, the heard and the unheard, and the perceived and the non-perceived in the dream state. In short, the mind is the one in control during the dream state and is able to perceive and experience things in a unique way that differs from the waking state.

5th Question

In the fifth question, Satya kaamah asks Maharshi Pippalaada about the significance of the word OM and how it relates to attaining virtuous human birth. Pippalaada explains that the word OM, also known as Pranava Shabda, represents the realization of the self and the supreme being as one and the same. He also mentions that even partial meditation on the word OM can bring enlightenment and ensure a virtuous human birth in the next life. Furthermore, Pippalaada explains that if one meditates on the first syllable "A" of OM with Rik Veda Mantras, it will bring about human birth and the possibility for self-control, meditation, and faith. If one meditates on the second syllable "U" of OM with Yajur Veda, it will elevate a virtuous person to the world of the moon and bring about human birth again. And if one meditates on the third syllable "M" of OM with Saama Veda, it will bring about unification with the sun and a purified and qualified pursuit of the supreme being. Pippalaada concludes that by properly utilizing all three syllables of OM, one can attain the ultimate goal of moksha, which is eternal and free from any suffering.

6th Question

The Sixth question, asked by Sukesha the son of Bharadvaja, is about the shodasha kalas, which are the 16 attributes or body parts of the subtle body according to Sankhya Jnaana. Sukesha was asked by a prince of Kosala Desha about the concept of the Purusha of shodasha kalas, but he didn't know the answer. He wanted to know from Pippalaadi Maharshi where that Purusha would exist.

Pippalaadi Maharshi explained that the shodasha kalas are not the ultimate reality, but are adjuncts to the body that are conditioned by ignorance. He explained that the true self is the Supreme and Absolute reality that is always present. He used the analogy of a lump of salt that dissolves in water and is difficult to retain its original form, which is similar to the human self that changes forms and names, but is still the true self. He reiterated the concept of Oneness and Unity rather than duality.

Summary

These six questions are all related to the nature of reality, the self, and the path to enlightenment. The first question deals with the creation of the universe and the methodology of realizing the ultimate truth. The second question deals with the prime supports of life and the concept of prana. The third question deals with the origin and destination of mortal life and what happens after death. The fourth question deals with the control of the body during the dream state and whether it is controlled by the mind or the soul. The fifth question deals with the significance of the word OM as a gateway to a better life and beyond. The sixth question deals with the concept of the shodasha kalas and the self, and how one can understand the true nature of reality through understanding the subtle body. All these questions are related to the ultimate goal of understanding the nature of reality and attaining enlightenment.

**"Om Bhadram Karnebhih Shrunuyaama
DevaahBhadram Pashyemaakshabhiryajatraah
SthirairangaistushtuvaamsastanoobhihVyashema
Devahitam YadaayuhSwasti Na Indro
VridhashravaahSwasti Nah Pooshaa
VishwavedaahSwasti Nastaarkshyo ArishtanemihSwasti
No Brihaspatir DadhaatuOm Shantih, Shantih, Shantih"**

The literal meaning of this mantra is: OM. O Gods! Let us hear auspicious words from our ears. O reverent Gods! Let us behold propitious visions from our eyes, let our organs and body be stable, healthy, and strong. Let us do that which is pleasing to the gods in the life span allotted to us. May Indra, inscribed in the scriptures, bring us fortune! May Pushan, the knower of the world, grant us prosperity! May Trakshya, who vanquishes enemies, bestow us with blessings! May Brihaspati bring us success!

OM Peace, Peace, Peace.

ॐ

V
Mundaka Upanishad

The Mundaka Upanishad is an ancient Indian scriptures that contain sacred knowledge. The Mundaka Upanishad consists of three chapters, each divided into two sections. The word "Mundaka" means "knowledge that liberates the mind from ignorance."

In this Upanishad, sage Angiras imparts to Shukra the knowledge of the supreme, beyond the limited knowledge of the tradition of the Vedas. The first chapter of the first section contains a discussion of the supreme knowledge in the form of a conversation between the sages and a description of the creation of the universe by the supreme being and ultimate realization of the supreme being through knowledge of the supreme (Para-Apara Vidya).

The second section discusses the necessity for the union of the guru and the qualified student for the attainment of the supreme being, the importance of sacrifice and its fruits, and the need to renounce enjoyment of the senses to attain knowledge of the supreme.

The third chapter, in the form of questions and answers, describes the path to realization of the supreme being through the path of the sages, who have reached the state of unity with the supreme being.

This Upanishads contain a wealth of knowledge about metaphysics, self-realization, and the nature of the universe. The Mundaka Upanishad is one of the texts found within this corpus and is divided into two sections. The first section, called the "Nirukta," focuses on the nature of the self and the ultimate reality, known as Brahman. The second section, called the "Khila," provides examples of the relationship between the self and the universe, and how to achieve harmony with the ultimate reality. The Mundaka Upanishad is considered an important text for both Advaita Vedanta and Dvaita Vedanta, and is often quoted by scholars such as Shankaracharya and Swami Vivekananda, as well as Madhvacharya.

The Mundaka Upanishad teaches that the creator of the universe is Brahman, who is also known as Atharva, Angiras, Satyavah, and Angirasa. According to this text, the study of Brahman is passed down through the tradition of acharyas, or spiritual teachers. The Upanishad addresses the question of what knowledge can lead to understanding everything, and states that Angirasa gave the teaching of Brahman-Vidya, in which he distinguished between the higher and lower forms of knowledge. He called the higher form of knowledge "paravidya", which leads to the realization of the absolute reality, or Brahman. The lower form of knowledge, known as "avidya", pertains to the world of letters and rituals. The text emphasizes that the ultimate goal of human existence is to transcend the cycle of birth and death, and attain liberation through the knowledge of Brahman. The Upanishad advises that one should renounce the world and seek the guidance of a guru to gain this knowledge.

The national symbol of India 'Satyameva Jayate' is also quoted from this Upanishad. The first chapter of Mundakopanishad, the first section of the first chapter explains the tradition of Brahman Vidya and the second section explains the ultimate realization of the Brahman by shedding off the lower Avidya knowledge and attaining the Paravidya, the higher knowledge of the ultimate truth. It also explains how one can achieve liberation and the ultimate goal of human life which is self-realization and liberation.

**"Om Bhadram Karnebhih Shrunuyaama
DevaahBhadram Pashyemaakshabhiryajatraah
SthirairangaistushtuvaamsastanoobhihVyashema
Devahitam YadaayuhSwasti Na Indro
VridhashravaahSwasti Nah Pooshaa
VishwavedaahSwasti Nastaarkshyo ArishtanemihSwasti
No Brihaspatir DadhaatuOm Shantih, Shantih, Shantih"**

The literal meaning of this mantra is: OM. O Gods! Let us
hear auspicious words from our ears. O reverent Gods! Let
us behold propitious visions from our eyes, let our organs
and body be stable, healthy, and strong. Let us do that
which is pleasing to the gods in the life span allotted to us.
May Indra, inscribed in the scriptures, bring us fortune!
May Pushan, the knower of the world, grant us prosperity!
May Trakshya, who vanquishes enemies, bestow us with
blessings! May Brihaspati bring us success!

OM Peace, Peace, Peace.

৪৩

VI

Mandukya Upanishad

The Mandukyopanishad is part of the Atharvaveda. It describes the supreme Mandukyopanishad' to Brahman, the Supreme Self, and its various aspects and proportions. The three matras, A, U, and M, and the three charanas, Vishvavara, Tejas, and Pragya, are mentioned in the fourth charana, which is without matra. It also describes the manifest form of the Supreme Self, Vishvarupa. The world is its abode, the seven Lokas are its seven limbs, and the senses, Prana, and Antahkarana are said to be its head. The path of worship of both the unmanifest and manifest forms of the Supreme Self is revealed in this Upanishad.

This Upanishad is the smallest of all the Upanishads, and is attached to the Atharvaveda. It is listed as number 6 in the Muktika canon of 108 Upanishads.

The Mandukyopanishad is renowned for its philosophical

discourse, presenting its verses in the form of twelve stanzas, and being associated with one of the four Vedic schools. It discusses the concept of four states of consciousness; presents a theory of Brahman, which is described as being both complete and self-existent; and claims that Brahman is the Atman (self).

The Mandukyopanishad is also noted for its recommendation as an Upanishad of liberation, being one of the ten principal Upanishads, and occupying the sixth place in the Muktika canon.

The Mandukyopanishad explains on seven "limbs", each one symbolizing a different spiritual cosmic plane or Loka. The Loka represent increasingly higher spiritual planes of existence, culminating in the 7th and highest plane, known as Satyaloka. "Om", the sacred primordial sound of the universe, is used to invoke these planes and bring them into balance in accordance with their universal order. The spiritual energies represented by the Loka can be further activated through study and meditation.

**"Om Sham No Mitra Sham Varunah Sham No
Bhavatvaryamaa,Sham Na Indro Brihaspatih Sham No
Vishnururukramah,Namo Brahmane Namaste Vaayo
Tvameva Pratyaksham, Brahmaasi Tvaameva
Pratyaksham Brahma Vadishyaami,Rtam Vadishyaami
Satyam Vadishyaami,Tanmaamavatu
Tadvaktaaramavatu Avatu Maam Avatu Vaktaaram,**

Om Shantih Shantih Shantih"

Om. May Mitra bestow us with blessings, may Varuna
grant us favor, may Aryama show us kindness, may Indra
grant us prosperity, may Brihaspati bestow us with
wisdom, and may Vishnu, who has vast coverage, grant us
with his benevolence. We salute Lord Brahma and Lord
Vayu, the embodiment of Brahman. We speak with
integrity and truth, may it protect us and our teacher. Om,
peace, peace, and peace.

ॐ

VII

Taittiriya Upanishad

The Taittiriya Upanishad is an ancient Hindu scripture that is part of the Yajur Veda. It is a collection of teachings that provide insight into the nature of the universe and the soul. The Upanishad is divided into three sections, each of which contains a variety of mantras and hymns. The first section focuses on the nature of Brahman, the ultimate reality, and the second section focuses on the nature of the individual soul. The third section is a dialogue between a teacher and student, in which the student seeks to understand the nature of Brahman and the soul. Through this dialogue, the student is able to gain a deeper understanding of the relationship between the two. The Taittiriya Upanishad is an important source of knowledge for those seeking to understand the nature of the universe and the soul.

Taittiriya Upanishad is one of the oldest of the Hindu scriptures and provides a deep insight into the essence of

Hinduism. It explores the power of Brahman, the Supreme Being, and his relationship with the individual believer. It also explains the importance of ritual worship, meditation and chanting mantras, as well as identifying key philosophical ideas and exploring aspects of karma, reincarnation and ultimate liberation.

The Taittiriya Upanishad is part of the Taittiriya Samhita, a literary collection of Vedic rituals and teachings, which is found in the Yajur Veda. In the Upanishad, the main focus is on finding the ultimate essential truth, or Brahman. The Upanishad states that Brahman is the unifier of everything that exists, and that he is the unseen and unknowable absolute truth, beyond the boundaries of time, space and causation.

The Upanishad also explores the concept of karma, the law of cause and effect. It states that one's actions in this lifetime determine the course of their next life, and that one's future is determined by their past actions. It explains that by living a virtuous life and engaging in beneficial activities, one can gain good karma and move closer towards moksha, or liberation.

The Upanishad also explains the power of meditation and chanting mantras. It states that by focusing the mind on Brahman and reciting certain prayers, one can access higher spiritual understanding and benefit from the power of mantra. It also states that by repeated chanting, one can purify their soul and move closer towards spiritual liberation.

The Taittiriya Upanishad also explores the concept of

reincarnation, which it explains is a result of the accumulation of karma over multiple lifetimes. It states that one's accumulated karma determines the shape of their current and future lives. It further states that an individual's life is a cycle of rebirths, in which the essence of their existence is constantly changing, yet the soul remains the same.

Finally, the Upanishad explains that if an individual is willing to practice virtue and proper conduct, then it is possible to transcend the cycle of rebirth and achieve ultimate spiritual liberation. It explains that to do this, it is necessary to experience deep, profound love for Brahman and all forms of life, and to surrender fully to His will.

After all, the Taittiriya Upanishad is one of the most influential Hindu scriptures and its content and essence provide a deep insight into the philosophy and metaphysical vision of Hinduism. It explores the nature and power of Brahman, the importance of morality and rituals, and the idea of karma, reincarnation and spiritual liberation. Through its content and essence, the Taittiriya Upanishad serves as an invaluable source of wisdom and guidance to believers seeking an understanding of the spiritual realm.

"Om Vaang Me Manasi Pratishthitaa Mano Me Vaachi Pratishthitam Aaveeraaveerma Edhi Vedasya Ma Aanisthah Shrutam Me Maa Prahaaseer Anenaadheetena Ahoraatraan Samdadhaami Ritam Vadishyaami Satyam Vadishyaami Tanmaamavatu Tadvaktaaramavatu Avatu Maam Avatu Vaktaaram Avatu Vaktaaram Om Shantih, Shantih, Shantih"

The precise significance of this mantra is: OM. Let our words be rooted in our thoughts, and our thoughts be rooted in our words. May Brahman reveal itself to us and may we comprehend the truths of the Vedas. Let us not forget what we have learned. Let us dedicate both day and night to study. We speak with integrity, we speak with truth, and may it protect us. May truth protect our teacher.

OM Peace, Peace, Peace.

VIII

Aitareya Upanishad

Aitareya Upanishad is an ancient Hindu scripture that is part of the Rig Veda, and is believed to have been composed between 800 and 600 BCE. It is a collection of philosophical and spiritual teachings that explore the nature of the divine, the relationship between the individual and the divine, and the path to liberation. Aitareya Upanishad is one of the most revered ancient Hindu scriptures and contains a vast array of complex spiritual teachings.

The Rigvedic Aitareya Upanishad is the fourth, fifth, and sixth chapters of the Aitareya Aranyaka and is considered to be part of the Upanishads. The first chapter consists of three sections, while the remaining (second and third) chapters each have one section.

The first section of the first chapter outlines the concept of creation by the Supreme Being and the creation of

Lokapalas. It also describes the birth of Virat Purusha and the gods from Hiranyagarbha, as well as the need for a human body and food for the gods. The second section describes the creation of the eternal from the beginning for the gods. The third section describes the way in which the souls should receive other souls and enter the path of Moksha, as well as the need for the individual to recognize the Supreme Being in order to attain liberation.

The second chapter describes the experience of the life cycle by Rishi Vamadeva. It mentions the first birth of the being in the womb of the mother, the second birth as a child, and the third birth as death through the Yonis to come outside world.

The third chapter answers the question of who is the worshipper by establishing that the Supreme Being is the only one to be worshipped. After attaining this knowledge, one can attain the ultimate abode of immortality by sacrificing and renouncing the material world.

The three sections of this Upanishad conents a number of verses that discuss various aspects of the divine and the path to liberation. The first section focuses on the nature of the divine, the second section focuses on the relationship between the individual and the divine, and the third section focuses on the path to liberation. By summarizing the Aitareya Upanishad, readers can gain a deeper understanding of the ancient Hindu spiritual teachings and the path to liberation.

The Aitareya Upanishad is composed of three books, the Brahmana, Aranyaka and Upanishad, with each book discussing a different spiritual subject. The Brahmana focuses on the three Vedic gods, Brahma, Vishnu and Shiva, and their relationship to one another. The next book, Aranyaka, contains teachings on the various Vedic rituals and religious ceremonies that are to be observed in Hinduism. Finally, the Upanishad contains a collection of sacred sayings and teachings on Vedic philosophy, the nature of reality and the paths of liberation.

The Upanishad discusses the power of knowledge and how it can liberate one from the cycle of reincarnation. It suggests using one's knowledge and wisdom to attain liberation. Overall, the Aitareya Upanishad offers a powerful and detailed exploration of the spiritual and metaphysical concepts present in traditional Hinduism. The Upanishad's focus on various spiritual and metaphysical topics makes it an invaluable source of spiritual wisdom and insight.

"Om Aapyaayantu Mamaangaani
VaakPraanashchakshuh ShrotramathoBalamindriyaani
Cha Sarvaani Sarvam BrahmopanishadamMaaham
Brahma Niraakuryaam Maa Maa Brahma
NiraakarodNiraakaranamastva Niraakaranam Me
AstuTadaatmani Nirate Ya Upanishatsu
DharmaasteMayi Santu Te Mayi SantuOm Shantih,
Shantih, Shantih"

The Mantra implies: OM. May our organs, speech, Prana,
eyes, and ears be nourished and strengthened. The
Upanishads proclaim that the entire world is Brahman.
We do not reject Brahman, and may Brahma not reject us.
Let us strive to ensure that there is no rejection within us,
and let us focus on living a righteous life as prescribed by
the Upanishads. Be in us,

OM Peace, Peace, and Peace.

ॐ

IX

Chandogya Upanishad

The Chandogya Upanishad - a part of the Talavakara Brahmana of the Sama Veda is accepted as this Upanishad. It consists of 10 chapters. The last 8 chapters are taken as the Upanishad. It is one of the vast Kalewara Upanishads.

The Chandogya Upanishad is believed to have been written sometime in the 8th century BCE and provides an introduction to a complex system of mysticism and knowledge. It is structured in a dialogue between the teacher and the student, Uddalaka Aruni and Shvetaketu. Uddalaka Aruni is depicted as the guru, guiding his student on the path of knowledge and understanding the self. It is a dialogue between the teacher and student, but the teachings found throughout the text can be applied to all seekers of the truth.

The basis of this Upanishad is the Chandas, which is not

limited to literary composition but has a broad meaning. The meaning of Chandas is 'to be composed'. The poet uses a literary Chandas to express the truth and emotion. The letters, words, and syllables that compose the truth or emotion are the components of the literary Chandas. In the same way, the Rishi expresses the original truth through various means, and sees the composition of various elements of nature.

In the first chapter, the explanation of the Omkar has been given in the form of Rishi, Sam, etc. Understanding the mystery of joining the Omkar with the main Pranas through the utterance of Devasur Sangram, the spiritual and divine worship of Omkar has been clearly described in various forms.

In the second chapter, the description of various types of worship by joining Sam to Sadhak-Shrestha has been given.

In the third chapter, the description of the availability of various types of Amrita in different directions by calling Aditya as the honey of the gods has been given. Mentioning the authorities of this Madhavida, the similarity of Gayatri has been established and the direction of worship of Aditya in the form of Brahman has been given.

In the fourth chapter, the Brahma Bhodh is to be done by the Jabal, Agri, Hamsa and Mridag of Satyakam Jabal and the Upakhyan of the Upakoshal to be taught by various Agri. The fifth chapter is about Pran Vidya Park.

In the sixth chapter, the individualization of the Ashwapat and the Rishis in the conversation of Satyaketu and the

Prana of various nature is mentioned.

In the seventh chapter, the various forms of Ishwar and Atma have been clearly described from different perspectives.

In the eighth chapter, the worship of Brahman in various forms has been understood. In the ninth chapter, the importance of Tapa to acquire eligibility for the realization of Atma Tatva and Brahman Tatva through the story of Indra Virochan has been shown. Finally, the tradition of Atmajnana and its fruits have been described.

According to the commentary on the text by the philosopher Shankara, the Upanishad is divided into eight chapters and contains a total of 133 verses. The text is concerned primarily with the nature of ultimate reality and the means by which one can attain liberation (moksha) from the cycle of rebirth.

One of the key teachings of the Chandogya Upanishad, as expounded by Shankara, is the concept of Brahman, which is the ultimate reality and the ground of all being. Brahman is said to be without attributes or qualities and is beyond the reach of human understanding or comprehension. The Upanishad asserts that the individual self (atman) is identical to Brahman, and that realization of this identity is the ultimate goal of human existence.

Another important concept discussed in the Upanishad is that of the "chhandas," which can be translated as "meter" or "prosody." The Upanishad compares the chhandas to the breath and states that just as the breath is the life of the body, so too are the chhandas the life of speech. Shankara explains that the chhandas are not just the rules of poetry but they represent the "way of being" of objects and events in the universe. These are the cosmic order, the basic patterns of existence in the nature.

In addition to discussing these and other philosophical concepts, the Chandogya Upanishad also contains a number of stories and dialogues that illustrate its teachings. One famous example is the story of the boy Shvetaketu, who after being educated by his father, returns home arrogant and not understanding the true knowledge. He is taught by a sage named Uddalaka the true nature of self and the Atman.

The Chandogya Upanishad discusses the importance of the Om syllable, and how it is used in various ways, including for religious rituals and for meditation. It also talks about the concept of good and evil in relation to the Om syllable. It is said that the gods and demons both claimed the Om syllable as their own, and in the process of their struggle, the Om syllable became affected by good and evil. The gods then used it for different senses like smell, speech, sight, hearing and mind. The demons afflicted it each time and the result is that one smells both good and bad, speaks truth and untruth, sees good and bad, hears good and bad and imagines good and bad. However, when the gods finally revered the Om syllable as the life-principle (Prana), the demons could not harm it and they fell into pieces. The Upanishad states that this is because the life-principle is inherently good and free from evil. The Upanishad claims that Om is the symbol of the life-principle and all the organs in the body and senses of man reverence this principle, as it is the essence and the lord of all of them.

In the Chandogya Upanishad, in the eighth and ninth volumes of the first chapter, there is a discussion between three experts about the origins and support of the Om syllable and all of existence. The discussion was about the origin of the world and they come to the conclusion that it is space. They say that everything arises from space and goes back to space. Space is considered greater than everything else and is the final goal. The Upanishad states that Om syllable, which is considered the most excellent, is endless and whoever knows this and reveres the most excellent Om syllable, will win the most excellent worlds.

The tenth through twelfth volumes of the first chapter of the Chandogya Upanishad describe a legend that criticizes how priests go about reciting verses and singing hymns without understanding the meaning or the divine principle they represent.

The Chandogya Upanishad also describes the significance of chant, stating that the reverence for the entire chant is considered good for three reasons: abundance of goodness, friendliness, and wealth.

This Upanishad presents the "Madhu Vidya" on which it praises the sun as the source of all light and life and states it as worthy of meditation as a symbolic representation of the sun being the "honey" of all Vedas. The Brahman is stated to be the sun of the universe and the natural sun is a phenomenal manifestation of the Brahman. The text also extensively develops the simile of "honey", by describing the Vedas, Itihasa and mythological stories, and the

Upanishads as flowers.

The text also discusses the symbolism of the Gayatri mantra, which is the symbol of the Brahman, the essence of everything. It states that Gayatri as speech sings to everything and protects them.

The text also states that the ultimate heaven and highest world exists within oneself. The human body is the heaven world, and that Brahman (highest reality) is identical to the Atman (Self) within a human being which is the foundation of Vedanta philosophy. It offers proof that the highest reality is inside man, by stating that body is warm and this warmth must have an underlying hidden principle manifestation of the Brahman.

Chandogya Upanishad also describes moral conduct and ethical precepts that includes non-violence, truthfulness, non-hypocrisy and charity unto others, as well as simple introspective life. This is one of the earliest statement of the Ahimsa principle as an ethical code of life, that later evolved to become the highest virtue in Hinduism. The text asserts that the person who lives this way, will acquire a good reputation, and will not be harmed by others and will be protected by the gods and attain heaven after death.

Finally, the Upanishad unveils the essential unity of life and existence and urges humanity to seek the ultimate truth through meditation and reflection. It is by understanding reality and the nature of Brahman that one can experience liberation from the cycle of birth and death, and gain ultimate freedom from suffering and ignorance. In this way, the Chandogya Upanishad provides a unique and complex view of reality and our connection to it.

"Om Poornamadah Poornamidam Poornat
Poornamudachyate,Poornasya Poornamaadaya
Poornamevavashishyate,Om Shantih, Shantih, Shantih"

*The literal interpretation of this mantra is: That which is
Absolute, This which is Absolute, Absolute arises from Absolute,
If Absolute is removed from Absolute, Absolute remains.*

OM Peace, Peace, Peace.

ॐ

X

Brihadaranyaka Upanishad

The Brihadaranyaka Upanishad is a part of the Vajasaneyi Brahmana of the Shukla Yajurveda. It is called Brihadaranyaka because it was developed in both the Brihat (large) and Aranyaka (forest) sections. It consists of six chapters, each containing numerous Brahmanas. The Brihadaranyaka Upanishad is one of the most important and influential scriptures of Hinduism, and is considered to be the tenth in the Muktikā or canon of 108 Upanishads. Composed around the 7th-6th century BCE, this Sanskrit language text is contained within the Shatapatha Brahmana, which is itself a part of the Shukla Yajur Veda.

The first chapter contains seven Brahmanas. The first Brahmana (Ashvamedha Parva) describes the creation of a great Ashvamedha sacrifice, and the second describes the creation after the dissolution. The third describes the glory of the soul and its distinctions through conversations between gods and demons. The fourth describes the development of the four Vedas by Brahman in its all-pervading form. The fifth describes the origin of various foods, the importance of mind, speech, and life. It also mentions the importance of name and form and action.

The first Brahmana of the second chapter describes the dialogue between the young Garghya and the wise king Ajatashatru, which clarifies Brahman and the Self. The second and third Brahmanas describe the two forms of Pranopasana (Murta and Amurta) of Brahman. The fourth Brahmana is a Yajnavalkya-Maitreyi dialogue, which is almost the same as in Chapter 4, Brahmana 5. The fifth Brahmana describes Madhuvidya and its tradition.

In the ninth chapter of the third section, Yajnavalkya is questioned by various tattvavettas in the yajna of King Janaka. Gargi asked two questions, the first of which Yajnavalkya stopped by saying that she would fall into a pit. With the permission of the assembly, she asked two more questions and, upon finding the answers, told the people that no one could defeat her.

In the fourth chapter, there is a conversation between Yajnavalkya and King Janaka, as well as a friendly conversation between Yajnavalkya and the assembly. At the end, there is a tradition of this episode. In the fifth chapter, various forms of Brahman worship, along with the worship of a pleasant man and a Vak, are mentioned. With the death of Udhrvaga, the worship of food and various forms of life is understood. In the Gayatri worship, the fourth step is also mentioned with the three steps of Japa. In the sixth chapter, the excellence of life, the Panchagiri, knowledge, the science of Mantra and the science of progeny are described. Finally, the tradition of all the teachers is mentioned at the end.

The first chapter of the Brihadaranyaka Upanishad begins by exploring one of the many Vedic theories of the creation of the universe. It posits that before the universe began, there was nothing, and then Prajapati created the universe from this nothingness as a sacrifice to himself, infusing it with Prana (life force) to maintain it in the form of cosmic inert matter and individual psychic energy. However, the Upanishad goes beyond this, asserting that the world is not only composed of matter and energy, but also of Atman or Brahman (Self, Consciousness, Invisible Principles, and Reality) as well as Knowledge.

The Brahmana 4 of the first chapter then proclaims the non-dual, monistic metaphysical premise that Atman and Brahman are one and the same, with the idea that since the universe emerged from nothingness when the only principle that existed was "I am he," the universe continues to exist as "Aham brahma asmi" (I am Brahman). In the last Brahmana of the first chapter, the Upanishad explains that the Atman (Self) is revealed through being self-evident, through empowering forms, and through action (the work of a living being). The Self, the Brihadaranyaka Upanishad states, is the imperishable one that is invisible and concealed, pervading all reality.

The second chapter of the Brihadaranyaka Upanishad begins with a conversation between Ajatashatru and Balaki Gargya on the theory of dreams. They posit that human beings see dreams entirely unto themselves because the mind draws in the powers of the sensory organs, which it releases in the waking state. This empirical fact suggests that the human mind has the power to perceive the world as it is, as well as fabricate the world as it wants to perceive it. The struggle man faces, according to the Upanishad, is in his attempt to realize the true reality behind perceived reality - Atman-Brahman, which is inherently and blissfully existent, yet unknowable due to its lack of qualities or characteristics.

The fourth brahmana of the chapter presents a dialogue between Yajnavalkya and Maitreyi on the nature of love and spirituality, and how it relates to Atman. Yajnavalkya states that one does not connect with or love forms or the mind, but rather the Self of one's own and one's beloved. All love is for the sake of one's Self, and the Oneness one realizes in the Self of the beloved. He asserts that this knowledge of the Self, the Brahman, is what makes one immortal, and that all longing is the longing for the Self, as it is the true, the immortal, the real, and the infinite bliss.

The fifth brahmana of the second chapter introduces the Madhu theory, giving this section of the Upanishad the ancient name Madhu Khanda. The Madhu theory is one of the foundational principles of Vedanta schools of Hinduism, as well as other āstika schools of Indian philosophies. Madhu literally means honey, or the composite fruit of numerous actions on the field of flowers.

The third chapter of the Brihadaranyaka Upanishad is a metaphysical dialogue between ten ancient sages, exploring the nature of Reality, Atman, and Mukti. Paul Deussen likened the presentation of ancient scholar Yajnavalkya in this chapter to that of Socrates in the dialogues of Plato. The chapter presents the theory of perceived empirical knowledge using the concepts of graha and atigraha (sensory action and sense), listing eight combinations of graha and atigraha: breath and smell, speech and name (ideas), tongue and taste, eye and form, ear and sound, skin and touch, mind and desire, and arms and work respectively.[The sages debate the nature of existence, and whether any graha and atigraha prevail after one dies. After ruling out six, they assert that one's ideas (name) and one's actions and work (karma) continue to affect the universe.

The fourth brahmana of the third chapter asserts that it is the Self which is inside all, and that all Selfs are one, both immanent and transcendent. The fifth brahmana states that profound knowledge requires one to give up showing off their erudition, and instead adopt a childlike curiosity and simplicity, followed by becoming silent, meditating, and observant (muni), thus beginning the journey towards profound knowledge and understanding the Self of things, where there is freedom from frustration and sorrow.[28] In the sixth and eighth brahmana of the third chapter in Brihad Aranyaka Upanishad is the dialogue between Gargi Vachaknavi – the female Vedic sage – and Yajñavalka, on the nature of the universe.

The seventh Brahmana of the Brihadaranyaka Upanishad discusses the interconnectedness of the Self with all organic and inorganic beings, as well as the entire universe. It asserts that the Self is the inner controller of beings, intertwined with the interaction of nature, psyche, and senses, often without the knowledge of the individual. This Self is the true essence, and the ninth Brahmana, the longest of the third chapter, introduces the neti, neti principle, which is discussed later, along with the analogical equivalence of physical features of a man and those of a tree, with the root of a man being his Self.

The last hymns of chapter 3 in the Brihadaranyaka Upanishad also attest to the prevalent practice of the ascetic life by the time it was composed in the Vedic age of India. It is these ascetic circles that are credited for major movements such as Yoga, as well as the śramaṇa traditions later to be called Buddhism, Jainism, and heterodox Hinduism.

The Upanishad poetically compares the destruction of a tree to the death of a man, asking who is supposed to beget him anew. It then goes on to proclaim that Brahman is bliss, knowledge, and the highest good of one who gives charity and also of one who stands away and knows it.

The fourth chapter of the Brihadaranyaka Upanishad begins with a dialogue between King Janaka and Yajnavalka. This chapter delves into the concept of the Self, its various manifestations, and its implications on soteriology. The Upanishad states that the Self manifests in human life in six forms: Prajna (consciousness), Priyam (love and the will to live), Satyam (reverence for truth, reality), Ananta (endlessness, curiosity for the eternal), Ananda (bliss, contentment), and Sthiti (the state of enduring steadfastness, calm perseverance).

The Upanishad then explores the question of what happens to the Self after death, and provides the basis for two major themes in later Hinduism: the concept of the Self as individual selves (dualism) and the concept of the Self as

One and Eternal, which neither comes nor goes anywhere, because it is everywhere and everyone in Oneness (non-dualism). This chapter also discusses the widely cited neti, neti, not this, not this) principle in one's journey to understanding the Self.

The third brahmanam of the fourth chapter examines the premises of moksha (liberation, freedom, emancipation, self-realization). This section contains some of the most studied hymns of the Brihadaranyaka Upanishad, which Paul Deussen calls "unique in its richness and warmth of presentation, with profoundness that retains its full worth in modern times."

The fourth chapter of the Brihadaranyaka Upanishad also features the widely-used greeting of Namaste, which is a common practice in Indian culture. This chapter provides a comprehensive exploration of the concept of the Self

The fourth brahmanam of the Upanishads' second section continues to build upon the thematic description of Atman-Brahman (Self) and the state of self-realization as achieved. Yajnavalkya declares that Knowledge is Self, Knowledge is freedom, and Knowledge powers inner peace. In hymn 4.4.22, the Upanishad states, "He is that great unborn Self, who consists of Knowledge, is surrounded by the Prânas (life-force), the ether within the heart. In it (Self) there reposes the ruler of all, the lord of all, the king of all. He does not become greater by good works, nor smaller by evil works. He is the lord of all, the king of all things, the protector of all things. He is a bank and a boundary, so that these worlds may not be confounded. He who knows him (Self), becomes a Muni. Wishing for that world, mendicants leave their homes."

The fifth and sixth chapters of the Brihadaranyaka Upanishad, known as the Khila Khanda, are considered to be a supplementary section or appendix. With the exception of the fourteenth brahmanam, each of these brahmanams is relatively small. According to Paul Deussen, this section was likely written at a later date in order to clarify and add important ideas that were relevant to the time.

The second and third brahmanams of the fifth chapter contain ethical theories, while the fourth brahmanam of the same chapter asserts that empirical reality and truth is Brahman. In the fourth brahmanam of the sixth chapter, rituals between a husband and wife are described in order to conceive and celebrate the birth of a child. These rituals are seen as a way to honor the divine and to bring joy to the family.

At its core, the Brihadaranyaka Upanishad is a dialogue between Yajnavalkya and his students. Here, Yajnavalkya advocates a spiritual approach to life that values reflection and contemplation over action. He teaches that human beings are composed of three distinct entities: Atman (the soul or self), body and mind. He emphasizes the importance of inner peace and encourages his students to release their attachment to the physical world in order to gain spiritual insight.

Throughout the Upanishad, Yajnavalkya distills various aspects of philosophical truth. For example, the concept of Atman is explored—the Upanishad explains how the individual self is a reflection of the divine, eternal being.

It further details the concept of maya, or illusion, and emphasizes the idea that the physical world that we experience is an illusion. The Upanishad also touches upon a number of other concepts, such as karma, dharma, and moksha.

The Brihadaranyaka Upanishad was composed over 2,600 years ago but is still read and studied today. Its timeless wisdom and insight into the relationship between human beings and the divine make it an essential part of Hindu philosophy. Through its teachings, it encourages us to ask the essential questions of life and discover the truth of our existence. The text encourages us to explore our inner depths and attain ultimate peace and contentment. The Brihadaranyaka Upanishad thus serves as an invaluable source of enlightenment for seekers of truth.

Summary

The Brihadaranyaka Upanishad is one of the oldest and arguably most well-regarded of the Upanishads, which has a large collection of various teachings and talk for achieving spiritual wisdom. The Brihadaranyaka Upanishad tells the story of two sages, Gargya and Yagvalkya, who have a dialogue about the nature of Atman. In this dialogue, Yagyavalkya explains that the Atman is inside of each of us and is eternal and indivisible. He further goes on to say that one must realize the true nature of oneself in order to find deeper meaning in life. Gargya then responds with agreement and questions if one can still attain moksha if their worldly desires are not fulfilled. Understanding these concepts allows us to move closer to realizing our divine potential. The conversation between

Gargya and Yagyavalkya has significance even today as it helps us understand how important it is to understand one's own inner self and its relationship with the world outside. This particular Upanishad focuses heavily on an Ashvamedha sacrifice, or a ritual in which horse sacrifices were offered.

OTHER BOOKS OF THE AUTHOR

1. The Moments When I Met God
2. Kashiyile Theertha Pathangal
3. GURU GYAN VANI
4. Abhiprerak Gita
5. ASSI SE JAIN GHAT TAK
6. Hopelessness of Arjuna
7. The Soul and It's True Nature
8. Sense of Action (Karma)
9. Action through Wisdom
10. Action through Wisdom
11. THEORY AND PRACTICAL OF EVERY ACTION
12. LOGICAL UNDERSTANDING OF THE SUPREME
13. THE IMPERISHABLE SUPREME
14. Yatra Nishadraj se Hanuman Ghat Tak
15. Yatra Karnatak Ghat se Raja Ghat Tak
16. Yatra Pandey Ghat se Prayagraj Ghat Tak
17. Yatra Ranjendra Prasad Ghat se Dattatreya Ghat Tak
18. YaatraSindhiya Ghat se Gwaliar Ghat Tak
19. Yatra Mangala Gauri Ghat se Hanuman Gadhi Ghat Tak
20. Yatra Gaay Ghat Se Nishad Ghat Tak
21. MAA GANGA, GHATEN EVM UTSAV
22. Ganga Arti Dev Deepavali evam Any Utsav
23. Potentials of Digitalized India
24. VEDIC CONSCIOUSNESS
25. A Brief Introduction to Vedic Science
26. Kashi ke Barah Jyotirling
27. IMPACT OF MOTIVATION
28. Let's have a Milky Way Journey
29. Color Therapy in a Nutshell

30. Rigveda in a Nutshell
31. Yajurveda in a Nutshell
32. Samveda in a Nutshell
33. Atharva Veda in a Nutshell
34. Ayushman Bhava - Ayurveda
35. Srimad Bhagavad Gita and Upanishad Connection
36. Srimad Bhagavad Gita - an attempt to summarize each chapter.
37. Facts and Impact of Nakshatra
38. Astro Gems - NAVARATNA
39. Ekadashi - A Concise Overview
40. A Concise View of Hanuman Chalisa
41. Inspirational Gita
42. Nakshatraranyam
43. Summary of 18 Mahapuranas
44. Synopsis of 18 Upa Puranas
45. Rigvediya Upanishads
46. Shukla Yajurvediya Upanishads
47. Krishna Yajurvediya Upanishads
48. Samavediya Upanishads
49. Atharvavediya Upanishads
50. The Seven Great Sages
51. From Rocket Scientist to President Dr. APJ Abdul Kalam
52. The Visionary's Voice - Quotes of Dr. APJ Abdul Kalam
53. The Wisdom of Swami Vivekananda: Insights and Inspiration from a Legendary Spiritual Teacher
54. Ayurvedic Remedies from the Garden
55. Sages and Seers
56. Rising Strong – Motivational Stories of Women
57. Beyond Flames -Mystery stories of Funeral Ghat Manikarnika
58. The Origins of Tulsi: A Look at the Mythological Roots of the Plant"

59. The Holistic Cow: A Look at the Physical, Spiritual, and Cultural Importance of Cows in India
60. Arts of Healing
61. Exploring the Divine
62. Understanding Five Elements
63. The Etymology of Ram
64. Symbols of India
65. Voice of Change (About Speeches of Great Men)
66. She Speaks (About Speeches of Great Women)
67. **Patriotism on Celluloid – Brief About Patriotic Films**
68. **The Music of Motivation: A Brief Guide to Inspirational Film Songs**
69. **Unlocking the Secrets of the Dashopanishads**

Contact

DR. JAGADEESH PILLAI

PhD in Vedic Science

Four Times Guinness World Record Holder

Winner of Mahatma Gandhi Vishwa Shanti Puraskar and
Global Peace Ambassador

Gemology, Astro & Vastu Consultant - Spiritual Counselor

Consultant for designing World Record Ideas

Efficient Tarot Card Reader

9839093003

myrichindia@gmail.com

drjagadeeshpillai@facebook

drjagadeeshpillai@instagram

jagadeeshpillai@youtube

www. JAGADEESHPILLAI.com

ॐ

|| LOKAHA SAMASTHAHA SUKHINO BHAVANTU ||

• 85 •

|| LOKAHA SAMASTHAHA SUKHINO BHAVANTU ||